The Vikings

Written by Sally Hewitt

W

FRANKLIN WATTS

LONDON•SYDNEY

First published in 2006 by Franklin Watts
338 Euston Road, London NW1 3BH

Franklin Watts Australia
Hachette Children's Books
Level 17/207 Kent Street, Sydney NSW 2000

Editor: Rachel Tonkin
Designers: Rachel Hamdi and Holly Fulbrook
Picture researcher: Diana Morris
Craft models made by: Anna-Marie D'Cruz
Map artwork: Ian Thompson

Picture credits:
British Museum, London/HIP/Topfoto: 27; Werner Forman
Archive: 13; Doug Houghton/Topfoto: 10b; Chris
Lisle/Vikingskiphuset, Oslo/Corbis: 8bl; National Museum of
Iceland/Martyn Chillmaid: 19t; Picturepoint/Topfoto: 8tr; Greg
Probst/Corbis: 15t; R. Sheridan/Ancient Art & Architecture
Collection: 26; Ted Spiegel/Corbis: 12; Ted Spiegel/Topfoto: 22t;
Statens Historika Museum, Stockholm/Werner Forman Archive: 7b,
10t, 16tr, 18, 22b, 24, 25t; Tim Thompson/Corbis: 14; Universitetes
Oldsammlung, Oslo/Werner Forman Archive: 7t; Viking Ship
Museum, Bygdoy/Werner Forman Archive: front cover t. ©York
Archaeological Trust: 20, 21t; Felix Zaska/Corbis: 16bl.

All other images: Steve Shott

With thanks to our models: Taylor Fulton and Ammar Duffus

Every attempt has been made to clear copyright.
Should there be any inadvertent omission please
apply to the publisher for rectification.

A CIP catalogue record for this book
is available from the British Library

ISBN-10: 0 7496 6499 1
ISBN-13: 978 0 7496 6499 2

Dewey Classification: 948'.022

Printed in China

Contents

The Vikings

The Vikings came from Norway, Sweden and Denmark. These were countries surrounded by sea and covered in forests. They lived near the coast and were fishermen, farmers and **craftsmen**.

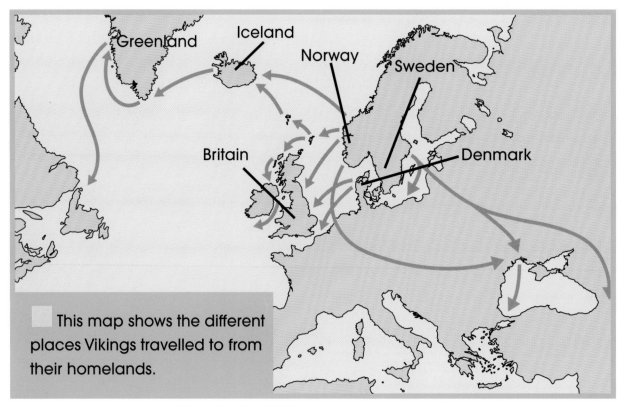

Greenland
Iceland
Norway
Sweden
Britain
Denmark

This map shows the different places Vikings travelled to from their homelands.

Raids

Viking warriors crossed the seas in their **longships** to Britain and the Mediterranean. They went up rivers into Russia and to faraway Iceland and North America. They carried out **raids** for money, treasure and **slaves**. They also went looking for new places to **settle**.

Settlements

The Vikings settled in the places they **conquered**.
They farmed and fished, and traded with local people.
The Viking period of raiding and settling started in the
8th century and lasted for about 300 years.

How do we know about the Vikings?

Graves and **burial ships**,
hoards of buried treasure
and signs of settlements all
tell us about the Vikings.
Historians wrote about their
conquests. Viking **myths** were
passed on by storytellers.

A Viking carving from a
church in Norway.

This weathervane
would have originally
been displayed on a
Viking warship.

Sea journeys

The Vikings were expert sailors. Not only did they build strong, fast ships, they also knew how to find their way using the sun and the stars to guide them.

Longships

The Vikings built longships. These could survive long journeys in stormy seas full of dangers such as icebergs and whales. Large sails caught the wind. Oars were used for extra speed and control.

This warship has been built as it would have been made in Viking times.

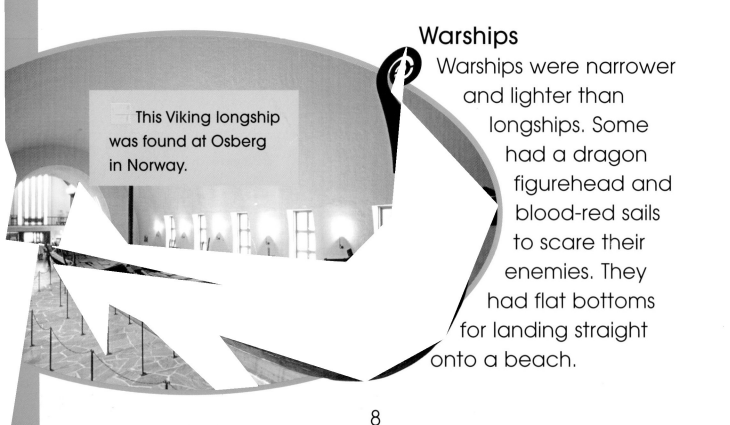

This Viking longship was found at Osberg in Norway.

Warships

Warships were narrower and lighter than longships. Some had a dragon figurehead and blood-red sails to scare their enemies. They had flat bottoms for landing straight onto a beach.

Make a model Viking warship

▶ **1** Draw the outline below onto a piece of folded A4 card. Draw the bottom line along the fold. Cut out the folded card and glue the shapes together at the very edges.

fold

▶ **2** Cut a rectangle of card 25 cm x 4.5 cm for the floor of the ship. Snip 2 cm tabs at each end and make a hole in the middle for the mast.

2 cm ⟶

▶ **3** Put a blob of Plasticine in the centre of the bottom of the ship. Push the floor shape into the ship and glue the tabs to the inside of the ship. This makes the floor of the ship. Paint the ship brown and add any details, like the dragon.

▶ **4** Cut out and paint 10 oars and 12 shields following the patterns shown.

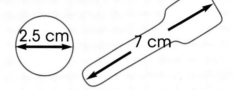

2.5 cm   7 cm

▶ **5** Glue six shields on each side of the boat. Make small cuts between each shield and slot the oars into place.

▶ **6** Paint an 18 cm x 16 cm piece of card red and white for the sail, punch a hole in the centre top and bottom.

▶ **7** Push a plastic straw through the holes in the sail, and then push into the Plasticine in the base of the ship.

Warriors

A Viking warrior was expected always to be brave and act like a hero. He had to follow his lord on a raid or expedition at any time. He was probably a farmer or fisherman when he was not fighting.

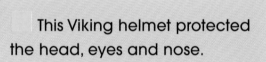

This Viking helmet protected the head, eyes and nose.

These men are dressed up as Viking warriors in battle.

Weapons and armour

Warriors were armed with spears, axes, bows and arrows, and swords. They were protected with round, wooden shields and metal or leather helmets. Wealthier warriors wore chain-mail shirts and carried finely decorated swords.

Make a Viking helmet

Make a simple helmet from papier mâché.

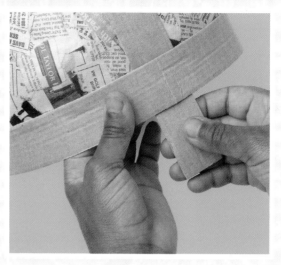

▶ **1** Blow up a balloon about the size of your head. Smear the top of it with Vaseline.

▶ **2** Tear up small pieces of newspaper. Dip them into a bowl of PVA glue diluted with water and cover the balloon with the strips of paper. Layer the strips thickly to make a helmet shape. Let it dry and then burst the balloon.

▶ **4** Add a nose guard. Paint your helmet in a metallic colour.

▶ **3** Glue a band of cardboard around the rim and across the middle of the helmet.

Viking raids

Viking raids were fast and fierce. They depended on surprise and speed. Warships appeared suddenly from the sea, giving the people no time to hide or escape. Warriors fought anyone who tried to stop them, stole treasure, took slaves and left as quickly as they had arrived.

A Viking sword like this one was a warrior's most valuable possession.

Ransom

The raiders sometimes took **ransom** money from terrified townspeople in return for a promise to leave them in peace.

Holy treasure

Monasteries and churches had treasures that made them a target for Viking raids. The Vikings stole money given as gifts, gold and silver **chalices,** and even bells.

Lindisfarne

In 793 CE, Viking raiders attacked the Christian monastery at Lindisfarne, an island off the east coast of Britain. Christians everywhere were shocked to hear that the monks had been killed or taken as slaves and the church's treasure stolen.

The ruins at Lindisfarne stand on the same spot as the monastery raided by the Vikings.

Lindisfarne monk

Imagine you were a monk at Lindisfarne and tell the story of the Viking invasion. Draw a picture to illustrate your story.

I was walking along the beach after morning prayers. I looked out to sea and saw a strange sight. A dragon's head rising out of the waves.

Viking houses

Most Viking people lived on farms and in villages by the seashore and in the countryside. People lived in **longhouses**.

Longhouses
Longhouses had one long room for living and sleeping in. Benches for sitting and sleeping on lined the walls. Meals were cooked on an open fire in the centre of the room.

This reconstruction shows the inside of a Viking house.

Building materials
Buildings were made of whatever materials could be found nearby. The walls were made of stone or wood. Sloping roofs were covered with strips of mud and grass called turf, or were thatched with reeds.

Outhouses
Houses were surrounded by small buildings used as workshops and storehouses. During cold winters, animals were brought inside to keep them warm. Some longhouses had a room alongside the living quarters for the animals.

Towns

Seafaring Vikings usually built their towns on the coast or by a river. Fishing boats and trading boats carried goods in and out of busy ports. Narrow streets were lined with small houses packed closely together.

A Viking longhouse.

Viking village

Make a model Viking village of small modelling clay buildings on a painted base.

▶ **1** Use the bottom of a cardboard box to make a base for the village (about 30 cm x 30 cm).

Paint it green and brown for the land and add a blue river or bay.

▶ **3** Arrange the models on the base. Put the longships on the water ready to go on a raid or trade voyage.

▶ **2** Make a longhouse, smaller houses, workshops and longships from simple modelling clay shapes. Score on details with a modelling tool and paint.

15

Daily life

Viking families living in the countryside had to farm or hunt for their food. They made their own clothes and tools.

Men were farmers, builders and metalworkers. When the men were away fighting, the women ran the farms and households.

Women combed their hair with combs made from bone or antlers.

Food

Vikings baked bread from flour, peas and pine bark. Meat and fish were salted or smoked to stop them going bad and stored for the long, snowy winters.

Hunting

When a **moose** or deer was hunted and killed, everything was used. The meat was eaten, the skin was made into clothes, and the bone carved into pins and combs. The antlers were used for spear heads.

Vikings wore simple but colourful clothes.

Clothes

Women **spun yarn**, wove cloth, and sewed and embroidered clothes. Children learned skills by watching and helping their parents work.

Dress up as a Viking

Children wore tunics – the same as their parents. Brooches and belts and pins held their clothes in place.

▶ **1** Fold a large piece of plain material in half, such as an old curtain.

▶ **2** Measure out a rectangle, making sure the top is along the fold. For a boy, the length is from the shoulders to the knees. For a girl, make the length from the shoulders to the ankles. It should be as wide as your shoulders.

▶ **3** Cut a semi-circle in the middle of the fold for your head to go through and then cut out the tunic.

▶ **4** Simply put it over your head and fix a belt around your waist to hold it in place. Add a brooch or pendant to finish it off.

Viking crafts

Viking **smiths** made weapons, tools and beautifully decorated plates and jewellery from iron, lead, gold and silver. They made silver coins for trading. Wood and stone were carved with detailed patterns, letters and stories.

Warfare

Well-made weapons, armour and ships helped to make the Vikings successful warriors.

Cloth

Women spun yarn from wool and then wove it into cloth. They made clothes and decorated them with embroidered borders.

Viking women and girls sewed delicate tapestries like this one from Sweden.

Loom

Most houses had an upright loom which was used to make cloth. The loom had long threads running from top to bottom. These are called the warp. Threads woven from side to side are called the weft.

Vikings used a large loom like this one to make cloth.

Weaving

▶ 1 Snip about 15 notches along the short ends of an A4 frame of card. The notches should be exactly opposite each other.

▶ 2 Wind wool for the warp around the frame, using the notches. Secure the wool so the warp is tight.

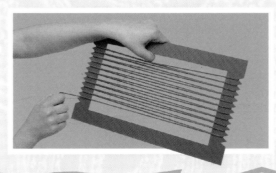

▶ 3 Thread a length of wool onto a big, round-ended needle for the weft.

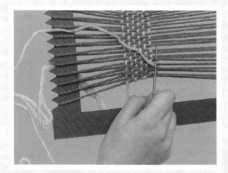

▶ 4 Weave the wool over and under from side to side.

▶ 5 Cut and finish off by tying the warp loose ends to make tassels.

Pastimes

Village chieftains held feasts that could last for a week to celebrate religious festivals, weddings and funerals. Eating and drinking was followed by stories, music and entertainment provided by jugglers and jesters.

Stories

Stories were not written down. Storytellers often sang their tales or told them in rhyme which made them easier to remember. They thrilled their audience with legends of the gods and the adventures of kings, chiefs and brave warriors.

Sport and games

Board games were played indoors. Outdoors, during snowy winters, people went skiing, skating and sledging.

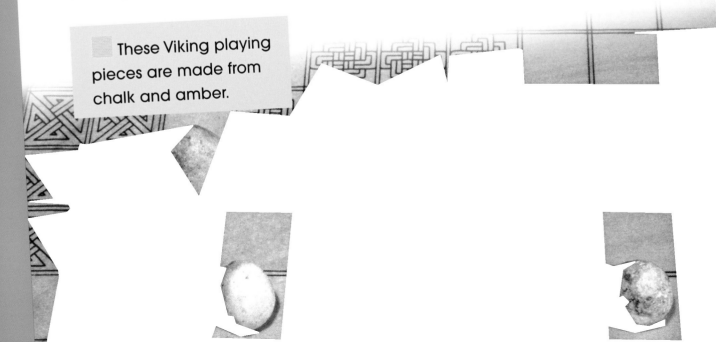

These Viking playing pieces are made from chalk and amber.

Music

Stories were sung to lyre and pipe music. Pipes were made from bone and wood.

A set of pan pipes was found at York – a Viking settlement – made from holes bored into wood.

A pan pipe and Viking whistles. Each hole in the pan pipes played a different note.

Make Viking pan pipes

▶ **1** Snip eight art straws into slightly different lengths. Arrange them by length from the shortest to the longest and tape firmly together.

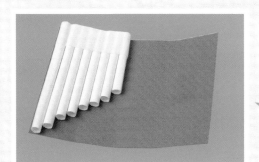

▶ **3** Fold the card round the straws and glue it down. Blow back and forth across the top to hear the notes.

▶ **2** Glue the straws onto a rectangle of thin card. Make the card as long as the longest straw and a little more than twice the width of the straws stuck together.

Life and death

Stones mark out the shape of a ship over this Viking grave.

The Vikings were **pagan**. When wealthy Vikings died, they were buried in a ship so they could sail to the next world. They were buried with things they might need in the afterlife.

Graves

Ordinary Vikings were buried in the ground with jewellery, a sword or something that was important to them. These were called grave goods.

Picture stones

Picture stones celebrated someone's life after their death. They were put up in public places for everyone to see. They praised men for their bravery and heroic deeds and women for being good wives and mothers.

The Gotland stone tells the Viking story of Völund the blacksmith.

Runes

Some of the grave goods had Viking writing on them. Viking letters were runes. Runes were made of straight lines so that they were easy to carve onto things, such as stones. Runes and pictures told stories.

Runes were made up of straight lines so that they could be carved onto stone.

Design a picture stone

This stone shows the story of a hunt.

▶ 1 Draw the shape of the stone.

▶ 2 Decorate the edges with a pattern.

▶ 3 Tell the story in pictures. Remember, the pictures were carved in stone so make the shapes and patterns simple.

Gods and legends

The Vikings worshipped many pagan gods and goddesses. The gods and goddesses each had a different personality and special powers. When Vikings settled in places where the local people were Christians, they became Christians, too.

The Vikings believed the gods protected them from monsters and fearsome giants who lived in the underworld.

This is a pendant of the goddess Freyja. It comes from Sweden. Around her neck is a necklace.

Viking gods and goddesses

Odin was the god of war. Warriors who died in battle went to his castle called Valhalla. He rode a horse with eight legs. Each day, he sent out two ravens to bring him news of the world.

Freyja was the beautiful goddess of love and war. She could turn herself into a bird and fly.

Thor was the most popular god. He was the god of thunder and of ordinary people. He fought giants and monsters with his magic hammer.

Vikings often wore an **amulet** of Thor's hammer for good luck.

Make a pendant of Thor's hammer

Thor used his mighty hammer to kill giants and monsters. Vikings wore a Thor's hammer pendant to protect them and bring them luck.

▶ **1** Draw the outline of Thor's hammer on a piece of strong card and cut it out.

▶ **2** Wrap it in silver foil and make a hole in the top with a holepunch.

▶ **3** Use a modelling clay tool or a blunt pencil to score on a pattern.

▶ **4** Thread (silver) string through the hole and wear it around your neck.

Famous Vikings

The Vikings were great adventurers. Many of them are still remembered today.

Eric Bloodaxe

Eric Bloodaxe was the ruler of Northumbria from 946–989 CE. When he captured his enemy, Egil Skallagrimsson, he threatened to kill him. Egil persuaded Eric to spare him by writing a poem in praise of him. He said his poem would make Eric Bloodaxe famous forever. When Eric heard the poem he spared Egil's life. He is famous to this day.

A Viking axe had a sharp iron head and a wooden handle.

These are lines from Egil's famous poem:

On his gold arm
The bright shield swings:
To his foes, harm:
To his friends, rings;
His fame's a feast
Of glorious war,
His name sounds east,
From shore to shore.

Leif Eriksson

Leif Eriksson (975–1020 CE), a Viking from Iceland, was a great explorer who is said to be the first European to discover America. The remains of a Viking settlement have been discovered in Newfoundland in Canada.

King Knut (or Canute/Cnut)

King Knut was a Christian Viking. He was king of England from 1016–1035 CE. He is famous for standing on the seashore and trying to hold back the waves. He failed, but he did it to prove that God, who ruled the waves, was greater than any king.

William the Conqueror

William the Conqueror was king of England from 1066–1087 CE. He was from Normandy in Northern France, an area named after the Norsemen (Vikings) who lived there.

His ancestors were Viking invaders. He invaded and conquered England in the famous Battle of Hastings in 1066 CE.

This silver penny was made during the reign of King Knut.

Glossary

Amulet

An object worn to protect against evil.

Burial ships

Wealthy Vikings were buried in burial ships together with things they would need in the afterlife.

Chalice

A special cup used in Christian ceremonies.

Conquer

To attack a place and to take control over it.

Craftsmen

People who are skilled in making things.

Grave goods

Objects found in graves. Vikings were buried with grave goods to use in the afterlife.

Hoard

A secret store of gold, silver and other valuable objects.

Longhouse

A long building where Viking families slept, cooked, ate and worked together.

Longship

Viking longships were long and narrow. They had oars and one large sail.

Moose

A kind of large deer with big, flat antlers. Vikings hunted moose for their meat, skin and antlers.

Myth

A traditional story about gods and heroes.

Pagan

A pagan religion is one which is not Christian and in which many gods are worshipped.

Raid

A sudden, surprise attack to capture slaves or steal treasures.

Ransom

Money paid to the Vikings to stop them carrying out attacks.

Seafaring

Describes people who travel and trade by sea.

Settle

To find a new place to live.

Slaves

Slaves were owned by their masters and were not paid for their work.

Smith

A craftsman who makes and mends metal things.

Spin

To twist wool or linen into long, thin threads.

Yarn

A long, thin thread made by spinning wool or linen.

Index